Mad Habits of a Life

Mad Habits of a Life

Julie Chappell

LITERARY PRESS
LAMAR UNIVERSITY

ISBN:978-1-942956-65-5
Library of Congress Control Number: 9781942956655

Cover Photo: Dennis Jarvis

Lamar University Literary Press
Beaumont, Texas

To my husband, Hank Jones,
whose madness matches mine, perfectly.

Recent Poetry from Lamar University Literary Press

Bobby Aldridge, *An Affair of the Stilled Heart*
Walter Bargen, *My Other Mother's Red Mercedes*
Mark Busby, *Through Our Times*
Stan Crawford, *Resisting Gravity*
Chip Dameron, *Waiting for an Etcher*
Glover Davis, *My Cap of Darkness*
William Virgil Davis, *The Bones Poems*
Jeffrey DeLotto, *Voices Writ in Sand*
Chris Ellery, *Elder Tree*
Alan Gann, *That's Entertainment*
Larry Griffin, *Cedar Plums*
Michelle Hartman, *Irony and Irrelevance*
Katherine Hoerth, *Goddess Wears Cowboy Boots*
Michael Jennings, *Crossings: A Record of Travel*
Gretchen Johnson, *A Trip Through Downer, Minnesota*
Ulf Kirchdorfer, *Chewing Green Leaves*
Jim McGarrah, *A Balancing Act*
J. Pittman McGehee, *Nod of Knowing*
Laurence Musgrove, *One Kind of Recording*
Godspower Oboido, *Wandering Feet on Pebbled Shores*
Carol Coffee Reposa, *Underground Musicians*
Jan Seale, *The Parkinson Poems*
Steven Schroeder, *the moon, not the finger, pointing*
Glen Sorestad, *Hazards of Eden*
Vincent Spina, *The Sumptuous Hills of Gulfport*
W.K. Stratton, *Ranchero Ford/ Dying in Red Dirt Country*
Wally Swist, *Invocation*
Loretta Diane Walker, *Desert Light*
Dan Williams, *Past Purgatory, a Distant Paradise*
Jonas Zdanys, *Three White Horses*

For information on these and other Lamar University Literary Press
books go to www.Lamar.edu/literarypress

Acknowledgments

I would also like to express my gratitude to the numerous journals and anthologies that originally published many of these poems:

The Call of the Chupacabra
Concho River Review
Red River Review
Dragon Poet Review
Malpaïs Review
Scissortail Commemorative CD
Stone Renga
Voices de la Luna
Writing Texas

CONTENTS

III. Autumn—Bone Fragments

IV. A Winter's Tale

I.
Spring—
Wildflower or Weeds?

The Birth of a Poet

In loving memory of Jim Spurr

Aruru, great goddess of creation
threw a stone far out into the air
to create a special human unlike all the rest,
the stone flew until it splashed into the sea
stopping the currents, the tides, the movement of the waters
until
that stone began to turn into a man,
a small circle rippling out to the side,
then, another circle, a bit larger than the last
then another, larger still
and another
as a man formed from toe to top,
his eyes, his ears, his nose, his mouth
emitting poetry, the song of life, love, loss, and infinite wisdom
from deep within him it came flying out in droplets
across the endless ripples of his creation
until the world shook with his song.

"Live loud, live long," he said.
And we listened, enraptured, embraced by his mighty voice.

Before Pearl Harbor

In an old box camera black and white,
my father stands on a cliff in Southern California,
his young, vibrant self facing the sea,
his 1940's billowy trouser legs catching the breeze,
his young wife snapping the picture,
capturing his youth, this moment
for their, as yet, unknown children.

Though the day is dimmed by clouds covering the sun,
no shadows fall on their still bright future.
They explore the beach, the cliffs, their spirits filling
with youthful eagerness even as the engines of war,
prepare to destroy lives young and old,
on an island my father might even be imagining,
his eyes looking seaward from his cliff-top perch.

A few weeks more and the bombs will rain down
on that beautiful Pacific island, blowing ships and bodies from land and sea,
a half ocean away from where my parents smile
into the camera to hold onto fleeting moments of life,
ignorant that along that same California coast, too soon,
friends and neighbors will grow suspicious, distrustful of each other
as their government legalizes the seizure of goods, of human lives,
interned for the duration or forever if they don't survive
in concentrated spaces.

But for now, all that is unimagined by my parents
who will not, after all, make California their home
but will head back to their Midwest home,
my father to join up,
my mother to trade a home of her own for her parents',
my future forever altered with theirs.

B-mail

The word is out:
The sage is good at our house.
Everyday we add a bumblebee.
Up to four now . . .
shaking and coaxing the pollen
out of every purple petal.

Like tiny black and orange hovercraft,
they float and glide from branch to branch
promising eternity.

Execution

I.

The rattlesnake's head separated cleanly
for his sins—
he had dead eyes
and a forked tongue
and slithered
and lay in the path of *rightwisnesse*.

At 3, I only knew
the swift flash
of my mother's hoe
as she brought down
her just punishment
on that which lay in our way
to the garden.

II.

The smell of Thanksgiving,
cherry, apple, pumpkin pies baking,
homemade bread toasting for stuffing,
my mouth watered for the lot.
But the dangers of a busy kitchen
were too much at 3, and I was shuffled off to be
with my grandmother in the next room
where she sat crocheting at the table
while I gravitated to the window as usual
to look beyond the garden.

But my eyes only reached to the edge of the garden
where my father stood

axe in one hand
head of a living turkey
against an old tree stump
in the other.

Without warning, the axe flashed,
the turkey's head separated from his long neck
and from the top of the neck, a fountain of blood
gushed forth while the turkey's body
pointlessly staggered here and there,
rooting me to my spot
witness to the execution of bird and baby ways.

Feline Profundity

If humans could understand themselves
as cats do when they are kittens

> hiding under mama's tits
> wrestling each other
> in fits
> and starts
> wandering beyond the edge
> of maternal salvation to
> make their biggest mistake . . .

trusting humans to understand what kittens can

that life exists to be inhaled into every pore,
exhaled over every distant plain
tasted, batted, jumped on, crawled into

until sleep overcomes us
and we drop in our tracks,
guiltless.

Crawfish Boil

Frowning and five-years-old,
I scream an alarum
from the dining room window
where I spot the flames
on the hillside.

Grandma, wheelchair-bound,
and I, too young to do anything
but fret and hold onto her chair,
watch from atop the basement stairs,
inner and outer doors open,
so we can see the burning grass beyond
where mother, sister, brother
beat the county fire trucks to the scene
beat the fire by hand
beat the flames into the creek
where it is swallowed up
extinguished,
heating the once-cool water
to the boiling point.

I wonder if the flames
in the water would boil
the crawfish that always pinched me
when I played along the water's edge.

Then I smile and turn away.

Evelyn Among the Great Writers

Whitman
Fitzgerald
Evelyn
Thoreau
Hemingway—

Evelyn?

Topps cards of
Great American Writers
pose along the top of a
small desk in front of
books, papers, hats, and jazz CDs,
the faces of the greats
and your lovely, little face
incongruous
among them.

E pluribus unum
yes, I've always thought of you as
one out of many, dearest Evelyn,
but one what remains to be seen;
you are, after all,
only 8 years old.

But what you've revealed in those eight years
places you less incongruous
among these great writers,
these performers of life.

At 2, you were performing
scenes from your imagination
in front of the mirror
your doting daddy

mounted at just your height
to indulge your already vibrant
natural performing spirit.

I came upon you there
in one of my all-too-infrequent visits
from that faraway place called Texas
and found you in front of that mirror
grimacing
contorting
mimicking
the facial and bodily expressions
of your elders
telling your own stories
in your pre-literate way.

In a Memphis Beale Street eatery and jazz club
you made a 3-year-old's beeline
for a stool and microphone
set up, but vacated
for Christmas Eve quietude
until a jazzman recognized
a kindred spirit in you
returning with his horn
blowing Memphis-style riffs
just for you.

This smiling third-grade-posed-picture face
conceals the blood bubbling in your veins
of artists, musicians, and storytellers
queuing up inside to help you
take center stage.

Condemnation

Holding the papers fast in his hand,
steady but solemn, the U.S. Deputy Marshall
walks toward the old farmhouse,
a sign of ancient pride and poverty
for the farmer who emerges,
stretching out his hand, cautious but friendly,
while the Deputy, my dad, feels the burn
of his duty in that handshake
and, watching, I feel condemned, too.

God's Chosen Ones

The laws of Moses inflexible,
purportedly made flesh, Truth
through later humanity,

none descended from Adam,
that apple-shaming prig,
instead descendants of that
long-lived, favorite son, Noah,
himself a literary theft from
Uta-napishtim the Faraway,
without Uta-na's gift of immortality
and with too many sons,
whose later wives' existence puzzles,
all other humanity having died in *His* Flood!

Uta-napishtim and his wife made
men and women by casting stones,
the bones of the earth, after *their* Flood.
Noah did no such heavy lifting,
and his wife disappears from the story
after Noah makes sacrifice for safe landing.
And which animals did he sacrifice anyway?
Wasn't the command to bring ALL the animals to safety?

Uta-napishtim, faulty like the rest of us, granted immortality.
Noah, deemed perfection, granted only a few extra years.
The point?

Alcatraz

At 8, I watch my father, return
from taking prisoners to Alcatraz,
bringing me a rock plucked from the Rock,
the little rock, bearing life
rather than taking it.

A creature had attached itself
firmly onto the rock's surface
its shell unbroken
in spite of a long journey
from Pacific sea of salt
to pacific sea of tall grasses.

I didn't know from sea creatures
so I filled the bathroom sink
with water from the tap,
plunged the rock into my sea,
the poor creature yet unseen
clinging for life
in that cold, fresh water
suddenly emerging like
Venus from her half-shell
a sea snail awaking
from its confinement
on the rock.

At 42, I move slowly,
deliberately with the crowd
tuned to the audio tour and walking
along the line of cells on Alcatraz,
empty now save for the paying customers,
the customers who paid with their lives
haunting us through earpiece echoes

of the Seven Deadly Sins
of every Commandment broken
of every social contract ignored
on both sides of the prison walls.

I think of my little rock,
that tenacious sea snail and my dad,
duty-bound to deliver himself, chained by law
and men convicted, shackled, chained by law
together, watching the scenery
from the windows of the car
carrying them all to the Rock
of temporary confinement for one
and permanent exile for the others,
tangible life slipping by
helped along by self-fulfilling prophecies
of poverty, perversion, pretense
of life and liberty for all.

These men shared with my father
the journey to this Rock
on which I now move
decades later
through the same spaces
they had shared
all of us listening,
time dissolved into sounds
of the real Alcatraz,
cell doors clanging
chained legs jingling
voices mocking in confinement,
for "99 years to Life."

A cruel irony
is confinement on that Rock
rising from a sapphire sea,

sparkling like the City
whose presence mocks them
as they watch
from the Rock
its wealth
its whiteness
its perversion
the City
atop a shifting plate of rock
ready to shake them all free
into that shark-infested Bay
together.

Stone Love

I broke the stones with my father's old hammer
each stone selected with care by my ten-year-old self
stones with quartz shards glittering
Fool's gold pieces glistening
ancient sea creatures fragmenting,
yet forever trapped in Kansas stone.

Stones collected with tiny sand dollars
from warm Pacific beaches
nestle in boxes and bags with stones
from pebbly sands of a cold North Sea
hundreds of lake and river stones
collected on family journeys here and there
ironically cover every spare surface
in my faux-stone house.

Chastised, ridiculed, mocked, and belittled
for my affection for stones
no one comprehending my love
of bits of earth and life passed on,
keeping me connected
to my past, to my future
as dust to dust
stone to stone
I become.

Sacrificial Lambs

Evil clothed in religion
is still Evil.

One by one or en masse
they send the young
armed with fear and false promises
and glory hereafter,
while the rhetoricians
stay back cloaked in their sanctity
their sorcery of words.

The Book open before them
armies of duped minds of innocents
bodies to follow
blinded by the Word in every language
arising from the throats
of false prophets
preaching war
justifying death
bearing hate
offering
the rightway to heavenward
to sit on the right hand
for rewards in the after life
that the innocents sacrificed
won't be able to contradict
in death.

Evil clothed in religion
is still Evil.

Beatlemania

Chaos reigned supreme
in the noise and melee of thousands
of teenage girls racing around empty chairs
looking for that precious vantage point
to see and be seen.

I stood, suddenly lost,
separated from my friends
on the field where a stage stood
ringed with stalag-like fencing,
those empty chairs filling fast,
and mine still unclaimed.

The cosmos, watching out for me,
pushed me nearly headlong into another girl,
also lost and searching,
a friend to share the chaos with.

Armored with our new-found friendship
our vision cleared, we found our seats
just before the Fab Four glided onto the stage.

Well-schooled by books and magazines,
radio and television,
a cacophony of high-pitched voices
called out, begged, pleaded for distinction
that the so-familiar harmonies
were muted to near extinction.

Later, we would claim to have
heard The Beatles play and sing
but what we heard were our own voices
raised high in worship to our gods,
alive for one night and
only a surging throng away.

Wildflowers or Weeds?

I look across my yard
and see delicate pink blossoms
in a little tasteful clump,
glories of the morning seeking
the sun
reflecting white,
subtle mauve.

Wildflowers?

Weeds! Say my neighbors.
Poison them!
Kill them!
They are uncontrollable!

I look down the street
and see soft, sky-blue clusters
of blossoms
wildly covering
another nearby yard.

Weeds?

Wildflowers! They say,
Protect them.
Spread their seed—
cover the earth with the only Blue
allowed in Texas.

From Martyrdom to Martyrdom They Fall

We had been to Allen's Drive-In
to see and be seen,
were seen and saw,
in our adolescent glee
until time called us home.

From the gate
I walked up the path
into the old house
expecting the smell
of my mother's baking or cooking
to lift me over the threshhold.

No such aromas arose,
no bread, no cookies,
no sauerkraut, no roast
no smells, no noise,
nothing met my seeking nose and eyes
except a note on the old oak table.

Grandma fell. We're at the hospital.

Grandma couldn't walk;
how could she fall from her wheelchair?
She needed my mother's guidance,
even to move from one throne to another.

The accidental nature of the fall
insufficient to assuage guilt long-placed,
part of my mother's very being
part of her mother's martyrdom
in mortal body crippled
by age, by genetic mutation,
an unquiet suffering

borne by my mother,
and carried still by me.

One Dying Day

I gaze at the family photo taken
the day of my grandfather's funeral,
January 29, 1954.

My brother kneels next to a cousin,
like the brother he never had, both boys
smiling out on this dismal day of loss,
happy in their camaraderie through life and death,
now, the brotherhood long gone
as loss of mind and body takes the cousin first.

Another cousin stands just behind
our grandmother's wheelchair, holding
tightly to it feeling the superiority
of her position among the cousins,
in her family holding sway by birth order,
if not by beauty and brains, all lost now
from disease unimagined then.

The toddler me sits in the middle
cross-legged, trying to smile
though pain of his loss unending,
one slightly older cousin, doll-obsessed,
holds one in front of her,
the irony of this yet to be known.

My parents stand near our canary's cage.

Is he singing on that day my mother
had dreaded for so many months,
as she tended, nourished, and loved
her father's dying frame?

Aunts, uncles, cousins, straining for a pose
surround the matriarch's chair,
conveying silent strength to those
gazing on her in the unfathomable future,
all the while the unsuspected void grows.

Scenes of Family Life

I close my eyes and
see my mother and her sisters
bustling about the old farmhouse kitchen.
It could be Thanksgiving, Christmas, Easter,
or just another Sunday family dinner.
I can't see myself to see
what age I am in this scene.
If I could I would know more
but still not what day gathers
the clan together around the
scents of roasting meats,
steaming vegetables, cooling pies.

No matter what day, I am sure
we gather for my grandmother,
the matriarch of this clan.
Does this scene I see,
precede the fall, the schism
that tore these women from my mother's side,
from her smiling contentment of family first?

They gutted her
with their greed
their selfish demands
for their rightful portions,
and nothing
was ever the same again.

Rattlesnake Redux

At 3, I only
looked on in terror
as my mother separated
the rattlensnake head
from his slithering body
in one fell blow,
the hoe slicing down
without hesitation
as one mother
protected her rattled child
from another.

Knowing it Took the Universe

True hope is swift, and flies with swallow's wings:
Kings it makes god, and meaner creatures kings
                    Richard III (1597)

Knowing it took the universe
billions of years
to tune a cat's purr to the right pitch
to perfect the mauvish pink color of a redbud's bud
to revive the death of winter to life in spring,
gives us hope that we, too,
might yet be tuned, perfected, revived.

II.
Summer—
Cicadian Rhythm

Shades of Summer Past

Shadow of a windmill
cast on cooling water,
sow with piglets threatening
two small children crying out,
one mother rescuing,
both protecting their young.

Birds and Boys

The male grackle spread his wings
shaking his tail feathers, his most impressive feature
as wide and fast as he could
to call a female,
any female, to him.

The boy expanded his chest
displaying his most impressive feature
shaking in the attempt
to attract a female,
any female, to him.

Birds and boys
shaking it,
getting low down,
and desperate.

Summer 1964

The girls lay bare-legged on the grass
having found at last the right spot,
where their transistor radio's static subsided
letting WLS-Chicago come in loud and clear.

They waited for a note
a signal
any one of a dozen favorites
over which they could argue
the precedence of John, Paul, or George—
Ringo adored by all but the true love
of none.

A field behind their houses
offered the least intrusion
from lights,
from brothers,
from static of any kind,
for one whole night
of communion with their gods.

Black and Blues

Albert Collins' guitar
winds through my subconscious
and I dance as I drive
running errands, daydreaming,
until his rough but melodic voice
cries out to his woman,
Gonna chuck a brick at you!

What?

He swears he will *hit her upside her head,*
violently blaming her,
less able to defend her body,
from yet another angry man,
becoming
another woman who will wear
the black and blue

while his chorus claims

You know I love you, you know I do,
you know I do, you know I do . . .

his violence fading with his voice
into the strains of woman's sorrow.

Cardinal Sin

The female cardinal alighted on the ground
at the foot of my little red oak tree
looking nervously about before she began
to feed on the seed that I'd scattered there.

Her mate, no longer content to wait
swooped down on her
sending her fluttering, startled
into the branches above.

Disillusioned at this mirror of human
selfishness and violence,
I turned away
feeling the universe shift,
yet again.

At the QT

If I could,
I would draw her—
high cheekbones
strong jaw
swirl of midnight hair
against skin like
whipped chocolate
a fierceness in her eyes
as she clutches
her little girl,
close to her chest,
a white bloated man
using his car
to push them
out of the way.

Global Warming

I

Dry creek beds abound
in this apocalyptic landscape,
drought haunting the land
summer and winter alike,
coyote, wolf, fox, raptor, prey
desiccated in guiltless sleep.

II

Water tumbles over banks
of creeks, streams, rivers now raging
vengeance of angry gods
summer and winter alike
coyote, wolf, fox, raptor, prey
submerged in human arrogance.

Tears of a One-eyed Woman

Driving to school this morning
where I will teach an ancient Egyptian tale
about a runaway servant of a Middle Kingdom pharaoh—
a proto-type for Job losing all only to gain back seven-fold—
I listen to Earl Hooker sing "Is you ever seen a one-eyed woman cry"
and tap my fingers on the wheel to his old-style bluesy beat
not really hearing the lyrics
until
I hear him proclaiming how she cries from her one eye,
just as I slow to turn a corner to see,
behind the wheel of a pale white pick-up truck,
a one-eyed woman waiting at the stop sign looking as unhappy
as near to tears as the one-eyed woman in the song must be
with a man who watches her cry as he "whips her" repeatedly
just to see that one eye crying
as the song fades . . .
"what a good woman, what a good woman, what a good. . ."

The Lottery

My Lai and the fall of Saigon were already history and yet young men, women, and children were still dying in Vietnam when the Nixon administration and its old, white men, reinstituted the draft lottery.

Young men and women holding their breaths on a college campus the day the numbers were pulled in March 1973, little blue capsules pulled from a bowl, like a number from a bingo roller or a raffle ticket for a year's supply of car wax, rather than for a life forever altered.

No one uttered the line that hovered in the air—"your number's up, man"—but it hung there, daring expression, the whistle in the graveyard of each boy's future, as it had been every year for the last decade, some boys long gone because their numbers were up, man.

The boys in that dorm room held tight to their college deferments while others their age, without the means or the desire, had joined up out of high school, or gone to work, or become fathers before their time, or already given their lives in the jungles and mountains of Vietnam.

Boys once sitting in high school government classes the last week of our innocence, announcing their upcoming departure to boot camp, bravely, ignorantly thinking they were saving us all, sacrificing themselves for liberty not lucre for the few whose sons never went, never were sent.

That March night, young men and women gathered tensely watching the television with so many lives at stake, wondering why birthdays had become a curse, hoping not to hear their own, their lover's, their brother's, their friend's, waiting, breathless to know who's next?

The Man in the Moon Grieves for his Mother

"Mon in the mone stond and strit"*   *stands and strides*
across the sky around his Mother Earth,
looking down in his slow progress,
grieving for her.

Mother, threadbare, is catching fire
while her resident, self-serving children,
who are not the Man in the Moon,
add fuel to the flames that burn her.

"It is much wonder that he ne doun slyt"*   *he does not slide down*
but holds firm above
not daring to take his eyes from his Mother
though he can pull the tides back and forth,
in and out, the water too seems alight
and cannot quench her flames.

Those other children stripped her of her abundance
to feed their own insatiable desires
though she had given selflessly and plentifully
they consumed without a thought for her
and the Man "shoddereth and shereth"*
at the sight of their neglect.   *shudders and veers*

As she burns, they poke and prod her
for nourishment she can no longer give
as they look to the Man in the Moon
their long neglected, unacknowledged sibling,
wondering as he goes behind the clouds of smoke,
"Whider trowe this monha the wey take?"*
                       Where, do you think, has this man gone?

The man, keening for his failing Mother, watches alone
as those other children tear each other to bits over her remains,

and, ungrateful to the last, pick her bones,
denying the true cause
of her wasting, of her dying.

Only the Man in the Moon grieves for his Mother
the others writhing in the mire of their selfishness
cry out
as Death refuses to hurry, to relieve their suffering
wrought by their disdain for the Mother of them all.

*Inspired by and these lines borrowed from the Middle English lyric, "Mon in the mone," c. pre-1350

Remembering a Man on a Hillside

I often wonder what became of that young, black man
sitting on the grass on a campus hillside
in early summer
so many years ago
wearing the comfortable clothes of our generation
enjoying the sun,
smiling

in spite of obstacles stacked against him
in spite of murderous prejudices
wrangled with
in words
in streets
in blood
there he sat,
smiling in the sunshine.

My gloomy twenty-year-old self,
returning after lunch to a detested job
feeling put upon,
passed him with head down,

he said,
"Smile! The sun is shining!"

Without thinking,
in spite of my native gloom
in spite of being no Pollyanna
in spite of an inability to 'look on the bright side'
I smiled.

He seemed to know
that he had touched me
that we would never meet again

that I would remember him
smiling, on that beautiful,
sunny summer's day
so very long ago.

Morning Rituals

A pigeon with cocoa-colored feathers
perches just on the other side of the glass
and cocks her head to one side,
expecting me to open the window
and sprinkle bits of toast along the ledge,
where she waits each morning for these
infinitesimal crumbs of bread,
smuggled off my breakfast plate
so we can share one moment of life
together.

Plesiosaur at Dusk

The blue whale dove nose first
into a sea of blue clouds;
in another moment
a plesiosaur rose
from the wisp of tail fin,
as we sat transfixed,
watching the ancient ones
rise again,
whale and dinosaur
made one
in a dusky, evening sky.

Tank or Pond?

Texas—manmade, earthbound watering holes
are called tanks.

Kansas—manmade, earthbound watering holes
are called ponds.

Kansas—aren't tanks
made from
metals and fibers
to roll over the 'enemy' in war
to be filled with fuel to roll down the road?

Texas—aren't ponds
framed in concrete
to stand knee-high to a mare
to be filled by metal pumps
powered by a windmill?

In unison—dig out the earth
wait for the rain to fall
to fill the hole, whatever you call it,
so animals can quench a thirst
so children can plunge into summer ecstasy
and watch the first tadpoles
hatch and hop
and fill the night air with their rhythmic bass
on the banks where the hot, dry earth
has turned
to cool, slippery mud.

A Taste of New Orleans with Tropical Storm Karen Blowing In

I am awash in poetic reminiscences
of poet-friends, my poet-lover
of our time in New Orleans when
tropical storm Karen threatened to blow us away.
All of us tourists chattered anxiously about the
dreaded possibilities while all round us
shopkeepers, waiters, night clerks in hotels
pedicab boys and winos on the street kindly reminded us
that they had survived Katrina, no other female storm
K or no K could hurt them now; they weren't budging.

The hotel in the heart of the French Quarter bustled by day
with fretful academics, half-sober businessmen, brides and their entourages
waiting for the night to bring music,
dancing, singing, laughter to disrupt the dead
some rode the carousel bar revolving nearly imperceptibly at night when
a cacophony of voices mixed with the music,
the tapdancing man, the less-rhythmic
brides, grooms, lovers, and strangers dancing, closing in on the performers
as if to consume their exhalations to preserve every moment
while New Orleans outside in its heart of hearts—
Royal, Bourbon, Iberville, Chartres—rolled on.

I can still feel the heaviness of the damp air in the morning
when the streets had been washed clean of the night before
when I walked down Royal Street for beignets and strawberries
when I wandered out at night for barbecue shrimp or gumbo to die for
when I revived by window shopping antiques and costume jewelry
when I listened to two young women playing violin and guiterne on the street
while people smiled, moved uninhibited, day and night
while my friend and I whisked along in the light of dark in a pedicab
driven by a young man talking exuberantly of his hope to write a novel
as he dodged the drunken girls who poked their asses out at us

stumbling and laughing while he deftly wheeled around them
sharing with us the vitality of a New Orleans night.

The taste of spicy brussels sprouts, étouffée,
red beans and rice, biscuits with chive and onion
linger-along with a place, a time I want to freeze frame
to return to when life-as-usual steals my lighter essence, weighs me down
to remember the bone-deep thrill of Kermit Ruffins playing his horn
telling his jokes, bringing his friends to the stage to play, to sing
to share the instruments of voice, piano, drum, bass guitar,
their New Orleans, their infectious delight and contentment
so that we knew they were doing exactly what they wanted to do
as they turned a multitude of individuals into one receptor
glowing in rhythmic happiness waiting for Karen.

Chupa Love

Chupa, chupa,

you fill my senses
hearing you
scratching
at my window
climbing in
reeking hot breath
on thin spread
covering my nakedness
whispering low in your throat
reaching for mine
baring teeth
tasting me
ravaging me
howling your victory
on the hill
above my life,

Cabra, cabra.

Only in Texas

There's another one.
Are you counting?

In the last ten miles, about ten dead armadillos.
Do you suppose there are any live ones in Texas?

Texas armadillos? Naw, they're just a myth.
Round midnight every night, there's a dead armadillo drop—
one little armoured body for every mile of highway.
Sure. They pick them up from one ten-mile section
drop them again the next night in another section.
Texas recycling and mythmaking all in one!
Saves time. Where are we headed?
I . . .

Bathtub on a pole!

What? Where!

About giraffe height wouldn't you say? Lovely shade of pink.
Why would you put a bathtub on a pole?
Well, my guess is . . . Camel!

What?

Camel, camel! Look right—camel!

What's it doing there?

Staring at the highway.

No! What's a camel doing in a little pen
near a highway in rural Texas!

Counting cars?
Boy, it looks really bored.

What time is it anyway?

Ten armadillos past a Texas camel.

Cicadian Rhythm

The trill of one cicada
rises and falls,
waits for an echo
to rise and fall, to wait.

I wander between the trees
disrupting the rhythm, stifling the echo
yet the caller tries again,
patient, knowing.

I understand now—
it's not *circadian* rhythms
that drive all organisms
into light and darkness and back again

but *cicadian* rhythms
the call and response of communion
of perpetuation of the species
of sex for life or for the moment.

I stand between the trees, quiet now,
marveling at the patience, at the persistence
of the caller, hoping in tune with him
to hear an echo rise and fall again.

III.
Autumn—
Bone Fragments

Mad Habits of a Life

A quiet unreality in this day
waits to leap out soundless
as you travel away from our home
and I remain
caught in the everyday
going about business-as-usual
expecting you at every turn
thinking already of ideas, questions, complaints
to mull over, to fuss about, to share.

What is it in our existence together
making you so necessary to my reality?

Your beauty, your body, your brains?
Your love of art, literature, music?

Yes. All of these.
And our mad habits of a life.

After all, it is hardly sunshine and roses with us,
more storm clouds and rosemary.

In the quiet, solitude long-looked-for
the unreality leaps out
tenacious
until your return.

As I Was Dusting

As I was dusting in my faux stone house
full of faux wood furniture
requiring no special oils
having no intricately carved pieces
no hand-hewn curves or lines
of honeyed oak or fine mahogany
I came to my lone piece of real wood—

The 100-year-old walnut treadle
Singer sewing machine that had
graced my late aunt's home
and her mother's before her,
still shining with the oil rubbed
generously over its thirsty wood.

I think of my aunt who gave this
to me when my first child was born,
hoping against hope that I would at last
become a homemaker
and stop having fancies about
reading and writing books.

I did sew one simple dress on this machine,
perhaps more to remind myself of my foremothers' labors,
women who either couldn't or wouldn't imagine themselves
striving in other ways to contribute to a larger world.
I thought it ironic for my aunt to see me as haus frau
when she had always worked outside her home.
She could not bear children to term so went out to earn,
to press her daily grief away.

I will pass this on to my daughter or my son
not because either of them will sew even one garment
but because they, like me, can feel family in that wood,
that walnut that shone as I was dusting today.

Ben Jonson and William Shakespeare

—a true tale of wit

Professor: The great English poet and playwright once said

Jonson: *"What the fuck! Which one of us are you talking about?"*

Prof: Oh, sorry. I'll rewrite.

Shakespeare: *"Never apologize, never explain!"*

Prof.: Right. Ahem. The great English poet and playwright, William Shakespeare once said—

Jonson: *"Really? You're going to call him, this so-called poet of Caliban and that usurping dipshit Prospero, the great—*

Shakespeare: *"Ben, let her proceed."*

Jonson: *"Who are you trying to kid, Shakeshaft? We know you're just going to steal a plot and make it so brilliant that no one remembers it was NOT your original idea."*

Shakespeare: *"I warned you and your bullshit attitude, Jonson. You trying to tell me that Volpone, that slimy faux-Italian villain isn't your theft of my most amazing Iago?"*

Jonson: *"Stop your bear-baiting, you son-of-a-Glover!"*

Shakespeare: *"Bricklayer's bastard."*

Jonson: *"Pompous ass!"*

Prof.: Boys. Seriously. You mustn't—

Shakespeare: *"You ARE Falstaff, you corpulent pig! You know that!"*

Jonson: *"You remember my Ursula, the pig woman at the Fair? Yeah, that's right. Your Mama."*

Shakespeare: *"Me thinks you doth protest too much, Biach."*

Jonson: *"Right. Fuck your chicken-shit, melancholic Prince and his cowardly sword-through-the tapestry. I'll run you through that smug little snatch on your chin!"*

Shakespeare: *"You and what Norwegian army?"*

Prof: I thought the pen was mightier than the sword?

Jonson & Shakespeare: *"Who asked ya!"*

Driver's Ed

Today, I pulled up behind
a police car at a stop sign sans signal
at this T intersection
so I wondered—
is he going to drive
straight into that house across the street?

Suddenly just as he was turning—
yes, he was turning—
he put on his signal.

I fumed at his neglect
because I like to know in advance
who to shout at for bad driving.

Then I realized
police working now
missed Driver's Ed!

They came of age
after schools began
cutting the "inessentials."

Well, I'm here to tell you
that Driver's Ed is essential,
it's critical!

No driver seems to know
what that little lever
on the steering wheel does.

Rules of the road? What are those?

Sure my generation said:
To hell with rules!
Down with the establishment!

But, Driver's Ed—
a rite of passage
to learn to

signal at least 100 feet before a turn;
keep a distance of 1 car length for every 10 miles per hour;
don't pass on a hill!

And don't even get me started about what happens at a 4-way Stop!!

Driver's Ed,
another abandoned child
of a self-serving system.

Eve #Metoo

We shall eat the apple in the nude
reconnecting with our inner Eve
but this time we will not share it.

We are *SURE* the Worm was Adam.

Haiku for Cats

Alex

Bird outside.
If not for the window
Breakfast.

Tommy

Greetings, you.
Mood switch mania
Slice.

Coey

Happiness everlasting.
Shark cartilage
Airborne.

Madison

Opaque green eye.
Kneel and serve
Aged privilege.

Bianca

Swift and silent
Streaking silver fear
Mythic promise.

Kitten

Catcophony of noise
Humans as chairs
Veiled contentment.

In the Footstepsnotes of Jesus

Footnote 1
> Virgin birth: Joseph was an illiterate carpenter who failed to ask pertinent, prenuptial questions.

Footnote 2
> Born in Bethlehem: Galilee or Judaea? The debate continues.

Footnote 3
> With the Elders in the temple: See "Home Alone 4: Lost in Jerusalem."

Footnote 4
> Water into wine: Wine disguised in a box painted with the Egyptian water sign unknown to the Hebrew celebrants.

Footnote 5
> Loaves and fishes: An al fresco parlor trick with baskets.

Footnote 6
> God incarnate: Bishops 297–Arius 3.

Footnote 7
> Fishers of men: Give it up, you can't catch fish in a Dead Sea!

Footnote 8
> The temptations in the wilderness: See Job.

Footnote 9
> The Last Supper: Jesus said "Bite me" to Judas which was misinterpreted by the other 11 disciples and perpetuated *ad nauseum*.

Footnote 10

'Crucified, dead, and buried, he rose again': See Footnote 5 with crosses, pomegranate juice, and stones instead of baskets of loaves and fishes.

Keith Jarrett and My Sister

Serendipity's a bitch
or a bastard,
you choose.
Keith Jarrett's piano riffs
sneaking into a quietly busy morning
as just another mishandling of my mobile
turns him on.

I start to protest by turning him off, to say,
"Not now, Keith, none of your grunting genius
right now."
And then my head receives the tune
clearly—

"Autumn Leaves"

my dad's favorite song
sung acapella by my sister
impromptu
over his soon-to-be descending
casket
over the gaping maw of his grave

me joining in as if
I had been the favorite.

Lament on Fire Ants

As I toil in my garden trying
to sift the dirt, displace the weeds
with new dirt and other less hearty green,
the damnable fire ants bite,
leaving snow-capped mountains of pain,
swelling and throbbing without cease.

I suppose I'll only make peace
with these busy, biting creatures
when I become dirt and weeds
in someone else's garden,
sustaining for eternity each generation
of fire-hot formica. [1]

[1]Formica is the Latin word for "ant." In the sixteenth century, Giovanni da Vigo (c. 1450–1525) in his *The most excellent workes of chirurgerye* (trans. from the Italian by Bartholomew Traheron [c. 1510 –1558?], i.ii. ii. 20v–21r., London: Imprynted by Edwarde Whytchurch, wyth the kynges moste gratious priuelege for seuen yeares, 1543 STC 24720), defined "formica" as a kind of abscess or excrescence on the skin, connecting it to its source, the ant: "Formica is a lytle pustle, or many pustles that come vpon the skynne. The thyrde [sygne] is pryckynge, and it is a sodayn bytyng as it were of an ante whereof it hath hys name."

Making Potato Salad

I made the potato salad
just as my mother had done
—almost—
switching her 1950s' Miracle Whip
for my 2000s' Vegenaise,
potatoes, eggs, mustard
all organic now,
hemp milk instead of
fresh cream from our own cows.

Would she have thought it domestic blasphemy or bliss?

Probably both—
just as she remembered
it and me.

The Lift

Glass boxes rise and descend
up and down
filling and emptying—
rich and poor
terror and calm
work and play
love and hate—
from floor to floor
lifting all
flawed and fallible
tainted and tarnished
banal and brilliant.

The Verge of Seas to Be[1]

I find myself making water features
in my kitchen sink
watching water rushing over the side
of a bowl bound for cleaning,
a waterfall that reminds me
of a seaside home left unwillingly
but necessarily long ago.

When I was 8, taking an infrequent turn at doing dishes,
I would while away the time by imagining
tales of sea foam and ocean waves
never seen from my midwest home,
where, later, I would write a story about a romantic sea voyage
with all that 12 could fathom, though still
without a whiff of salt air or a toe-touch to breaking waves.

At 18, finally taking my first breath of sea air,
my first sensation of sea on skin, I felt newborn,
staring out across the rolling, heaving water, wondering
who was looking East while I was gazing West beyond this shore.
A dozen years more and I would live an island life
surrounded by a Northwest sea,
realizing my childhood dreams of sea foam and salt air,

watching my children, small and fit,
piling sand on sand
digging moats and valleys,
eating hot dogs cooked over driftwood fire,
rushing hand in hand with me as the tide swooped back in
putting the fire out while
keeping our childhood dreams alight.

[1]This title is from the penultimate line of Emily Dickinson's "As if the Sea should part"

Vapors

When you awake
you will see that
the vapors of our anger
no longer hang in the air
but have vanished
like fog
with the rising sun.

Washing Up

I finish washing up as
my house fills with scents
of simple soup
of wholesome bread,
my thoughts turning from our plenty
to the dearth of so many others—
mothers, fathers, children denied
sustenance
facing starvation and brutality
while bloated politicians
spew rhetoric that reeks
and fill their overflowing plates,
to gorge on.

Dogankhamun

My old dog lying in an afternoon sun
so hot it would boil tar,
perhaps senses this
and rises to move to
a shaded spot on cool grass
then to another
until, inspired by
Akhenaten's holy disk,
she trots away
back into the sun
to sniff
to defecate
to run with agèd legs
made young again
in that Amarna-like sun.

Untethered

It's a *good day to die,*
the hospice voice rasped into my ears
already ringing with my father's rattling gasps
for air, for a bit more life.

Staring out at autumn blue
I saw, instead, a shroud of sky
a baldachin of grief.

Food they fed me didn't taste
Comfort they offered me wasn't
Hands they gave me were empty.

Air could not revive me
sun could not warm me
as flesh of mine died out.

I could do nothing but
hold his burning hand,
wipe his fevered sweat away

until I released his hand,
to let him go untethered
on that *good day to die.*

Bone Fragments

Robin's feathers sparkle in the sun
illuminating the far corner of my porch
where she stands quietly
atop the fossil rock resting there.

I wonder if she feels a kinship
with dinosaur bone fragments cemented
within the ancient stone—
does she sense the once green,
living grasses now long since
entwined with the bones of her ancestors?

Is it the stir I feel when I kneel
at the graves of my parents, my grandparents,
my kin who now complement
bone and plant and life moved on?

Or is it the ancient pull I feel
standing at the edge of the sea,
my toes touching earth and water
wind in my face sun blazing fire,
a feeling that I am
nearly home?

Two Poets Smoking Cigars at Twilight

For Ken Hada and Hank Jones

Two poets standing side by side smiling,
exhaling curling rings of smoke,
talking poetry, fishing, favorite cigars.

Keeping my distance
from acrid curls of smoke,
I share fishing and poetry,
and friendship in the day spent together,
walking, eating, drinking in the air,
connecting with Woody Guthrie's vibe
and each other's intellect and spirit,
settling now to the peace of the lake
the smoke carrying
our desires, our dreams, our hopes
to the gods at twilight.

The Revenant

The jalapeño pepper lay flaccid on the floor
impotent to save itself for better things.

Honky tonkers came in at the gentlemen's door,
stepping over the little bit of once shiny green,
once growing on a vine
alive and, by autumn,
full red it might have been
but for the hands that plucked it
as it basked in the summer heat.

This shiny green pepper stirred in with duller green
—avo and lime—
this little pepper might have been the heat,
the spark setting fire to a festive night
the light for an obscure romance,
the burn on a tongue quenched by salty margarita—

What a life it might have had!

Instead—
laying there
stepped over, neglected
not garbage, not food—

a revenant of heat,
cooling in the air.

Gardening with the Ancient Ones

I stand looking over my garden,
a profusion of periwinkles planted
by the fickle winds and fleeting birds
of many Texas winters.

The original red, white, and pink
merging over the years of windplantings,
scattering their seeds and those of
the multi-orange marigolds nearby
into an awe-inspiring ordered chaos.

Stepping gingerly into the garden toward
a slab of ancient flagstone, now bird feeder,
my feet suddenly subside into loose earth,
mounded over a subterranean passage.

I curse the gophers,
making their way beneath my garden,
but they are only returning to
their place of origin, their ancient home,
winter urging them to a long and guiltless sleep.

IV.
A Winter's Tale

A Winter's Tale

Outside, the snow glittered around the soda bottles
nearly buried in what had fallen,
was still falling, swirling around the glass
while inside
hot dogs blackened just so
by embers and flames
hedge and walnut blazed
in the old stone fireplace.

The child stood watching the night,
the snow swirling around the treat to come,
the half-frozen soda, the hot dogs,
the promise of flaming marshmallows after,
driving winter's despair
to the edges of infant consciousness
for one more, innocent year.

The "C" Word

When a doctor gave her
high-dose birth control pills
at 18,
to control pregnancy
he didn't say: "These might cause Cancer."

When a doctor advised a tubal ligation
to avoid continuing the same harsh birth control
at 28,
he didn't say: "These might cause Cancer."

When a doctor gave her
low-dose birth control pills
at 40,
to control erratic cycles,
he didn't say: "These might cause Cancer."

When a doctor gave her
estrogen supplements
at 50,
to control the end-of-things,
she didn't say: "These might cause Cancer."

When she found the lump in her breast,
not once but twice,
she asked the doctors, "Why?"
they only said: "The life-threatening drugs,
mutilating surgeries, scarring radiation
will delay your end but no guarantees for life."

These doctors, would not say:
"We have no idea how or why,"
but say instead:
"It must be something you did
or failed to do yourself."

94

Apostasy

My mother deserved
a long and healthy old age—
an octegenarian
running 10k's,
starting a career as a painter,
enjoying the absence of domineering husband
harping, demanding children.

But, instead,

year after year of increasing debilitation
shaking, waking, nightmares
fueled by Parkinson's drugs
until she was no longer able
to walk
to eat
to breathe
and
we had to say,
enough—
no more suffering.

And watch her slowly,
achingly slowly,
fade into death
begging her
to let go
begging her
to give up
begging God
to let her find . . .

Peace?

My father, her brothers, her sisters, her parents,
waiting in some conveniently familiar afterlife
on the right hand of God?

By the hand of God struck down?

Only God knows,
knows best
knows,
God?

bha cruinne ann uaireigin*

Once, people piled stones
5,000 years before the day
I walked round them.

Two Grey Cairns of Camster,
two mounds, one long, one squat and round,
a wooden walkway

keeping tourists alive,
off the boggy ground
to these chambers of the dead.

But the circle of stones nearby
has no walkway,
no sign to tell its story.

Not a closed circle this,
but stones laid intricately,
a three-foot gap facing East,
A ritual circle needing
the light of dawn in a place
where the sun rarely shines,

where the wind blows fiercely,
where torchbearers stood on projecting stones
ceremonial, funereal, sacrificial

humans and animals burnt within,
the moor holding its secret dead?

*the title is Scots Gaelic meaning "there once was a circle"

Christmas 1969

Seeking our Christmas tree, one cold night,
snow lightly fluttering in seemingly single flakes
across the rows and rows of leaning pines,
we wandered into a young man we knew
on his way to war but duty bound to find a tree
his infant son's first Christmas,
son and wife, the family waiting,
gathered together to celebrate the season
and his last days of life as usual.

Seeking our enemies over Quảng Ngãi
one hot, sticky morning, two months later,
this young chopper pilot's Huey lost oil,
lost altitude, began violently spinning,
crashing down, technology failing,
metal peeling, flying in single flakes on fire,
across the rows and rows of leaning banyans,
parasites at birth, growing in the cracks,
the crevices of their hosts, mocking
the natural order of things.

Eleven men KIA in a faulty Slick
while Nixon, Kissinger, other smug Suits,
called it a day within the hour of the crash,
carrying on as usual without premonition of losing altitude,
violently spinning or crashing down,
these parasites at birth, growing in the cracks,
the crevices of our land, mocking
the natural order of things.

Collapsing Allegory

The house leans slightly left
its eyes blank, glassless now,
no fire has charred its skin or
forced those within, out,
the detritus of its former life
blows in the fierce persistent
winds of winter threatening
to bring it down bereft of life support
around and about, in and out—
but stand it does on the lonely plains,
empty and hollow,
waiting.

Cuneiform

The darkness eases in
around the edges,
closes in on consciousness, and
swallows the single light
struggling to illumine the words
that transcend time
when darkness meant terror
and dawn the god's rising—
where fire
gave single light
to words pressed in clay.
wedge-words,
of power
of conquest
of pride
of divinity—
doom.

Dear Dad

I still can see
the ice-cold crystals of winter storms
swirling around the glass bottles
our treat
for being born to you
who never grew too old
for soda chilled in snow
or hot dogs roasted on the fire
or sledding dangerously, joyously
down the highest hill.

I still can see you
—long dead now—
blue eyes as clear to me
as when I saw them
lit up at the pleasures
of your children
drinking half-frozen bottles of soda
eating blackened hot dogs
screaming at the thrill
of another sled ride with you
even if now
only in our memories and dreams.

A Gothic Tale

The twists and turns
of bare winter branches
conjure up melodramatic scenes
far from this weeping redbud's
Spring-filled mauve-pink blossoms.

Deep-shadowed caverns and glowering revenants,
precipitous heights and ominous vales
prevail
as my tree and I
grow more crook'd and bent,
all too aware of the darkness rising round us.

North Star Muses

I write words—
on sidewalks
in the sand
in the air
on paper—
unable to resist
those nine magnetic goddesses
with their attractions
inevitable
irrestible
eternal.

On the Death of Two Cousins

One harbor sheltered us til now;
even as the lines aged and frayed,
they held, the boat still secure;
the sheet directed us leeward;
the rest, not yet ready
held fast to the mooring place.

But now,
I can feel the boat drift
slightly swaying.

As each line breaks,
I sense the unmooring to come.

The Plowman to his Progeny

Bless me Father,
Mother, Sister, Brother,
Daughter, Son, Lover,
Grandchild, Friend, Stranger.

For I have sinned.

It has been eternity since my last confession.

For a hundred million generations

I have Lusted after
the material and immaterial.

I have raised Greed and Gluttony
to an art form of obscenity.

I have fed on Envy
like a predatory beast.

I have wasted lives
in endless Sloth and indifference.

I have purged unselfish love
to frothing Wrath and rage.

I have preened my feathers
in pornographic Pride.

I have disdained the Humble.

I have undone the Chaste.

I have chided the Industrious.

I have fed on the Generous.

I have perverted the Abstinent.

I have ostracized the Charitable.

I have plagued the Patient to death.

No prayers can save You now.

Tremor

I saw a man this morning
walking down my street,
a bit unsteady but determined,
his baseball cap pulled down a bit
to block the January sun.

For that split second,
I thought,
it's our dear friend
coming by to see us,

but the split-second split open
like a fissure in rock
as the substance at my epicenter
trembled and shook
as the water gushed up and out
the natural fissures of my eyes

and I remembered—
our friend no longer
shares the everyday;
death holds him fast.

Yet, at my epicenter
his spirit holds and
cannot be shaken loose.

Stoned

Stones call to me
from where they lay
on earth
rock on rock
in sea
washed clean
reminding me
of where I'll be

Through the Looking Glass

My cat sits staring into the mirror
making grumbling noises.
I wonder if he's fussing at that 'other' cat
or is he, like me, disturbed, shocked
by the image that confronts him,
wondering where to find
that feisty *enfant terrible,*
that strutting, anguished youth?

My cat and I see all and none as, together now,
we squint into the glass, searching through time,
grumbling.

Then, tempting fate,
we run and romp,
we howl and prance,
dislodge our Selves,
evoking ages past.

White Noise

Mumblings and murmurings of nurses
couple with squeaky wheels
of infusion carts,
creating a kind of white noise
against the louder chorus of nurses
checking on, explaining to,
or comforting us, who are tied to chairs
by tubes with clamps and clear, dripping poison
running through them into us,
confined by our diseases.

We come willingly and not
since our choice is the proverbial
rock and a hard place—
poison that kills good and bad indiscriminately
or painful, dwindling death,
a choice we cannot bring ourselves to make.

So the chairs fill day after day,
with hope, laced with suffering and fear.

Winter's Cruel Intent

The sunflowers nod in October sun
and the bees sip from the sage blossoms
while I try to imagine winter's chill
descending, stifling these revels
until I realize that the plants
and bees must rest
in winter's cold embrace
as we, too, fall under the chill
of time, calcifying bodies
made too porous, too susceptible
to winter's cruel intent.

Confession

Like St. Augustine,
I have a confession to make.
I lusted, loved, and lost,
But, I didn't blame my mother.

That Friday Feeling

Students mill about outside classrooms
on this first Friday of the term;
it is January but the day promises warmth
and plenty of sunshine so
parties in and out of doors all night long.

My first sensation is weariness,
but as I rise in the elevator
their voices ride with me,
and I remember that Friday feeling
so long ago—

the anticipation
of friendships and flirtations
and downright simple good times
soaked with cheap beer,
the watery excuse
to rut and strut
to peer and leer
to see and be seen.

Daydream of an Afterlife

Since my last battle with cancer
I have been caught in the daydream of an afterlife
where my dear and departed family and pets
reside on the farm of my girlhood
where the silos and the sunflowers rise to the sky
where I ride my horse while my dogs run
and, because it's my daydream, all my quondam cats
prance merrily along behind horse and dogs.

In the old farmhouse my mother whistles and sings in her kitchen
joyously preparing to feed us all
and cousins, aunts, uncles, grandparents, friends,
whoever arrives and needs nourishment is welcome there,
or she is canning produce from her garden
or pears from our two small, abundant trees;
my dad sits near her at the old oak table drawing cartoons for the children,
or he is sitting outside creating—painting, carving, etching— happy in his art.

Here it is always summer, and the children run barefoot in cool grass,
or it is frozen winter but all revel contentedly on the hearth of a blazing fire,
laughing and living together in harmony that ever and never was or will be.

At the Edge

Sitting on the edge of darkness
dangling my feet.
reaching for the light,
watching the glimmering,
shimmering just beyond,
wanting to fall into it,
wanting to pull back
getting up off the edge
committing to nothing.

'Twas the Week Before Christmas

'twas the week before Christmas and all through the house
the poets were jamming and having a rouse
their words were ringing all through our ears
the better to segue to Salud and Cheers!

www.ingramcontent.com/pod-product-compliance
Lightning Source LLC
LaVergne TN
LVHW041323080426
835513LV00008B/567